I0483916

What Words Will You Leave Behind?

Written by Jo Grace

Published By

SMALL
BITE
BOOKS

Published by:
Small Bite Books^{Tm}

Email: graceupclose@yahoo.com

Written by:
The Graceful Communicator –
Jo Grace "Serving It Up In Small Bites!"
If you're like most, you don't have a whole lot of time, that's why I'm doing your homework, and serving up the knowledge in short written books!

Cover Designed by Small Bite Books

This book was produced from the numerous classes for adult learners, bible and aesthetic classes, book reports, lessons outlined, taught and studied by Jo Grace

Note to Readers
The words presented in this book have been inspired by years of teaching, and my own personal and spiritual development. I'm passionate about helping women discover their true value from within!

Special Thanks

To the Living Spirit of God
that resides within me.
Thanks to my Family & Friends
Loving me just the way I am! To
my daughters, and students.
**"The World Will
Miss Out If You
Don't Do You!"**

Thanks Jewel Diamond Taylor for
telling us "Don't give up!

TABLE OF CONTENTS

"To save paper we have tried to reduce
the extra blank pages."

Introduction

The Rewards of Writing

There's the thrill of the outcome, as you stand there holding a tangible item in your hand. Something that at one time was just a thought…you invested time and energy into making it happen. "A wish doesn't happen without action!"

If you are a speaker, educator, or coach, it adds credibility, and more than often depending on the content presented in your book, you will appear as the authority in your field of expertise.

Your book may be used to create an additional stream of income.

Your story in a written form can leave a legacy for your children, or it could transport your dreams into the future.

Maybe you're a thought leader, and you have an original idea that you want to promote. You may even have a dynamic presentation that could be monetized by turning it into a info-product (i.e. book)

Writing can translate your experience into a language that your audience can understand. You may, or may not be an expert on the subject that you choose to write about. But writing provides you the opportunity to share more information and options that may not be presented by an expert.

So What Are You Waiting For?

Are you waiting to become a good enough writer? Do you start but never finish? Maybe you think you don't have enough degrees, you're not smart enough. Well stop waiting... I'm sure there are books written by people who are less qualified!

You simply need to be smart enough to put your life experiences into a language that resonates with an audience. We all have lessons we've learned, and life degrees we've earned, that are worth sharing.

Or maybe you're the person waiting for more time.

More time, it's not gonna happen! You simply have to commit to scheduling it into your daily plan, or planner as an appointment with yourself & begin!

And this is why you want to partner up with a SBB writing coach, we help you through the process. You will learn how to create small, short attainable steps, on your journey to becoming an author.

If your goal is to write your 1st book, or create a series of books to sell at the end of your presentations... a Small Bite book writing coach can help you reach that goal.

Why are You
Reading this Book?

Well you just have to be smart enough, to know that the key is persistence. You have to keep at it, and make sure you're constantly pushing forward, believing in your work yourself, so you can accomplish the goal and reach the Dream.

Reading this book is a part of that push. Don't spend any more of your time talking about writing your book, write the book!

This book is research for you, showing you how to simply organize your information, and clarify it through small digestible bites. You can read other books such as Writers Digest, and any other variety of books to help you develop your writing style. You may even want to upgrade your grammatical skillsets...but don't become paralyzed, or immobilized by the fear of perfection. Practice makes us better, and each time you write a book you'll get better.

Breaking beyond the fear, all you need is a compelling idea, and an understanding of what you believe your audience would want to learn.

You probably already have a sufficient amount of knowledge on an area you wish to write about. Your SBB coach can assist you with the planning of your book outline.

Getting past the Blocks!

My writing has to be complex and sophisticated or I won't appear as an authority... this is certainly not true.

Most of the books written by very accomplished writers are written at a 9th grade level (75% of US adults read at this level), some of our famous writers have registered in at a 3rd grade level.

Content is King or Queen!

Great content is surely a must...but how easily your audience can comprehend what you've written is Key to how much our reader will retain.

The information you're providing has to be desirable and interesting, yet your reader should be able to fluently read what you have written; not having to stumble through or having to Google words they don't understand in order to comprehend what you're saying.

Our SBB editors will assist you with creating fluency with your sentences.

You won't lose your credibility by reducing the complexity of your writing... but you may actually gain more followers by reducing a complex subject matter into a simpler language that a larger audience can understand. They won't have to seek out a medical journal translator.

We want your readers to enjoy your writing, and that's why our editors make it a practice to read your writing with expression out loud in our focus group. Yours words should leap off the page at every turn, satisfying your reader's appetite in every small bite. After you create your draft, practice this technique, find someone who will actively listen and provide you with some great feedback.

What's Your Story Worth?

Now you can scratch off the fear of writing, because you're not sophisticated enough...or that you may or may not have gone to college. The real question is, "what is it worth to you?"...is it worth investing your time, energy, money? Is it worth sharing?

We all have a story, and your story could be a door opener to a speaking career. Speaking at the front of the room provides you an advantage that I call "Leverage at the Lectern."

You have the opportunity to touch, move, and inspire an entire audience...done right, they'll be ready to connect with you before you leave. If the event is organized properly you should sell a number of books at the back of the room.

A book is a novelty item, somewhat of a souvenir to mark an Aha moment for them along the journey; not to mention getting the author's signature.

If you do your follow through correctly you could build a database for a series of books, and open doors for more speaking engagements.

Your book can be used as a workbook, or be the lead step to your webinar, membership program, or an online training course.

If you're currently speaking on a regular basis without a book or infoproduct… you should ask yourself how much money are you losing?

Why Start Small?

Why set a small attainable goal? It's proven that once you accomplish something, you're more likely to do it again. Once you have the book in your hand, it will be proof of a completed project; filled with excitement at having accomplished your goal successfully you will be ready to rock n roll!

With an SBB coach you can make that happen in 30 to 60 days, a very short amount of time, and a small investment in comparison to what your return will be.

A small, but smart investment, that will bring you closer to becoming an author. You'll also have the option (with a completed book) to shop for an agent or publisher.

A small book is a short-cut to your dream of writing your 1st book, and an accelerated option for speakers, educators, and coaches desiring to create a product (infoproduct) which could lead to a passive income.

When you partner with SBB your plans are simply expedited, because you'll have a supportive team to keep you focus until completion.

Your book can be the driving force you need to move you closer to your purpose. Writing it could produce more meaning for your life, and impact the lives of so many others.

What's the Worst
Thing that Could Happen?

So ask yourself what's the worst thing that could happen if you write your book? What's the worst thing if you don't?

What needs to happen for you to take the next step? Are you ready to move closer to your dream of becoming an author? There are plenty of dreams buried in the graveyard of those who probably said "one of these days."

Whatever the excuse, you're the one deciding what the future will look like...will you leave any words behind? Will your words live beyond your lifetime?

A Success Strategy

Maybe it's an internal drive towards your personal success, and writing a book could play a big part of that.

Maybe you're seeking to attain a higher level of recognition for your work. Whatever it is that you wish to accomplish, writing a book can be a great strategy to get you there.

Books can help you build your brand, or even your tribe, but these are trade secrets we share with those who become SBB authors.

As an author one of your greatest strategies is public speaking, "Leveraging the Lectern."

Here is an opportunity to teach people about a facet of your industry, creating visibility as an "Expert" in your field.

Maybe you simply want to serve your community. With a finished book in hand, you can do that, and because of the relatively small investment required; not having to purchase a large inventory (to be stored in your garage), you can afford a supply of books as needed.

As an SBB author your books can be reasonably priced for an underserved community, and it's just economically smart; which is what we'll partner with you to teach in our "Short-Cut to Success" community workshop!

Maybe you want to empower others with your story. You may have a ministry or a niche that will impact the lives of women and their children.

Each time a woman (or man) finds the courage to share her truth whether its spoken or written, she empowers others with the seeds that she sows.

She's a "Carrier of Life", and her words produce freedom, and power! So here's the question again, "What Words Will You Leave Behind?"

Recently I watch a miniseries and the character said, "I will live, but my story will outlive me!" ~Book of Negroes. It was like confirmation for me.

You have seeds to sow!

I'm sure you've noticed our logo is an apple, and as the saying goes, "an apple a day, keeps the doctor away." Small Bite Books are great healthy Apple-tizers; with a strategically designed edited format for easy digestion, regardless of how sophisticated or complex the subject matter may be. Up for the challenge, with whatever ingredients are provided, our master chefs create a delicious, edible meal for all of you foodies out there.

Here's an advantage point of going small; a thinline book can be carried in a briefcase, purse, carry-on for travelers, and makes for an ideal read on the plane or train. Reasonably priced they can be gifted for Christmas stockings, or added to a Birthday basket.

Building your brand? They make great sponsor books to go into a gift bag at any type of conference.

Or maybe you have a philanthropic mission... your book could also be used as a fund raising strategy. If you happen to be the keynote speaker at a conference, you could donate all of your book sales made that day or split the profits. Guarantee they'll ask you back to speak again, and with a list of new purchasers you can increase your database.

You can use your book to build a membership ...and of course there are lots of other trade secrets, but we can't give them all away, some we keep in-house for our SBB authors.

If you're an author, we're here to serve you, and hopefully for those 1st timers...make that dream come true.

If you're reading this book you're ready for the next step...

What Should I Write About?

The topics to write about are obviously endless, but here are some things to think about:

What do you desire to write about?
Have you mastered an interest?
Can you express it passionately?
Can you write, sign, dictate, type?
What are you going to do with it?
What will your Bio say about you?
Will you share your personal story?
Are you ready for a writing coach?
Research needed for Facts, Images.

Think of people you enjoy being around, and share a common interest.

Your heart (emotional core), head (rational thinking), and gut (life preserver) must all be in harmony when you make this decision. Begin with the heart and the head in mind, but end with the gut, it'll never steer you wrong. It always has your best interest; your instincts will guide you, and the passion that it triggers will reflect in your writing.

Your hearts message will leap from the pages and land in your audiences lap; and they will read speedily through devouring every word. Your instincts and intuition combined with your intellect will take you where you want to go!

Small Achievable Goals!

Why are small achievable goals important?

The beginning of a journey starts with the first few steps. A child starts learning to walk by taking baby steps, and each step it successfully makes creates confidence to get up and take another, along with the encouragement of their parents cheering them on. And months later they're running around fearlessly as if they've been running for years.

SBB is here to cheer you on! Accomplishing a small goal set for you, such as writing a book creates a sense of success.

Success perpetuates more success, it promotes confidence, stimulates the imagination; creating a momentum, making room for expansion, and pushing the capacity of creativity.

In each of us there's an internal drive to succeed; yet success looks very different from one person to the next.

Success is not a destination, but it is one of those things that tend to continuously expand along the journey.

Success is simply accomplishing something that you deliberately set out to do.

It may be small daily goals, or it could be a lofty goal that requires more of your time, money and energy!

That which you've predetermined in your mind to do, and then you do it… is a successful accomplishment. Whatever small steps you take to make that happen will build your confidence, and writing a book could simply be a catalyst to that big dream.

The thrill of the accomplishment! Your enthusiasm, and excitement generated from completing this task will be contagious. Incorporating your book journey into your story could encourage others to write their own.

Perpetuating more Success!

Create a Series of Books from Your Blog!

Some of you may be thinking of having to start from scratch when you don't have to. If you have invested a number of years writing a blog, and or doing freelance writing...you're likely to have the foundational information you need to write a Small Bite Book. Here's an excerpt from "The Coaches Corner," from one of our contributing authors, Victor Irving Jenkins.

~ Process ~

While optimism has its perks, we do not always get the result we want. Not getting what we want is daunting and requires us to find a way to keep living until it surfaces.

My pastor once wrote a book entitled, What To Do Between 'I Believe and I receive' and its content ought to be noted. We are able to withstand nearly anything for one second, right, so we need only approach misery or disappointment one second at a time. After one gets a certain age, it is clear that all things work out in some way and even if it doesn't, we all die sooner or later. That may seem morbid but it really is good news. When you consider all the pain agonizing and suffering we do needlessly, knowing it all eventually ends no matter what we do is comforting. As a boy when I was punished by getting a 'beatin' it seemed the pain would never go away but it did go away eventually. Dealing with panic attacks for more than 8 years and now living without them convinces me that all things end in time and makes it very clear that the time spent agonizing is only useful because it got me from there to here.   And   being   here   Is   a   lot   of   fun. Enjoying the journey is more than just a cute saying. And as an extraordinary coach, you had better enjoy the journey so that your client will enjoy it too. If all things work together for good, then we must get very good at reframing everything. In coaching the operative question is always, "What's next?" And it can work in all areas of life. I spend some time in social media and have developed some relationships with people that do not always think the way I do. I have developed my thinking over the years and understand this process and have a much better handle on life than I used to. I see comments from people I admire and wonder what they could be thinking. I even have the nerve to become annoyed at times and wish they would be more like me.

The journey they are presently on looks a lot like my own journey did some years ago and it is almost predictable that they will come around. By come around, I mean they will come to the same conclusion I did. That conclusion borders on the fact that we can think about whatever we want to think about and we alone bear that responsibility. Just because I am there does not mean others do not have the right to make their own journey. I am getting much better at the old adage, "Live and let live." All I really must do is to wait and greet them with gladness when they finally get there.

I suppose there is a certain amount of arrogance associated with such an attitude. When I consider that the person who is offended is the one responsible for the assessment of arrogance, I feel much better about things. So what if I am perceived as arrogant? It is a very valuable asset in this case for it saves a lot of heartbreak anxiety about what is going to happen. Once you realize that all you feel results from what you think, you choose to think different thoughts. The sky is not falling...it is not going to be horrible...and you will find another job and a sweetheart nicer than the one you just lost. More than anything the idea of prayer makes us okay with whatever we are dealt. Even in the case of our children, we must be willing to weather the storm until they get to the other side.

Berating, and chastising and brow-beating might make you feel like you are doing something but there is more than talk to the saying "Love covers a multitude of sins." When the offense comes we must be ready. When we are called to watch someone get bruised, we must we willing to watch them heal. It is this mindset that is most helpful to the coach who is not getting the results she or he wants right now.

Get in the habit of staying until the end of the game because you never know what story to tell if you weren't there for the win.

Creating a series of books from what you've already invested time in writing, is smart marketing.

If you've been in the speaking arena for some time, I imagine you have a number of presentations. Here's an excerpt from a book of speeches.

~ Graceful Business Sense ~

The gospel does not provide an escape from reality or from the daily business of making a living. Rather the gospel connects us with God who strengthens us to take in life fully and completely!

While we serve God, not Mammon, that does not mean that we need to become impractical and useless. Jesus was a carpenter, Peter a fisherman, Paul a tent-maker. God's grace empowers, and strengthens you to cope with the outside world and it allows you to exercise dominion in it. You don't have to be a monk or a mystic. You can be a high-school teacher, a farmer or a master auto mechanic.

The gospel encourages personal vocation; daily work was seen as a gift from God whereby you actualized His will in His world. Work, particularly working quietly with one's hands is seen as a solid virtue throughout the New Testament. In the epistles, Paul exhorts them to lay aside idleness that came from being taken up with their dishonest ways and get down to providing for their daily needs in a constructive manner.

The apostle repeatedly takes pride in his own ability to work hard and provide for his own needs though he was entitled to ask for support from the churches.   (2 Corinthians 8 &9)

Those in Grace... will not gamble, believe in luck or let themselves be ruled by irresponsible and greedy impulses. Rather they shall cultivate the godly and righteous power to make wealth through the diligent application of specific and focused wisdom and knowledge towards a worthy economic goal. Thus they will refuse to operate in fear! ...afraid to charge a fee for your products or services... a workman is worthy of hire!

The renewed mind is a mind freed from the dominion of greed, idolatry, superstition and the search for luck. It is a God-centered mind that is quickened, intelligent, thoughtful and responsible and which applies itself to creative work for the glory of God. We move into economic blessing not by appeasing a host of minor spiritual beings but by playing by the rules of Almighty God and by diligently applying the wisdom He grants us to our lives.

~ These are just examples of the different options you have for gathering the content you need for your book. The message is yours, the story is yours.

Ok, one more example!

Here's a diary concept. Your journals could be filled with treasures, and great stories. And remember fiction or non-fiction the choice is yours.

Excerpt from ~ Born Woman
Born Woman maybe that's only unique to Me. Who else even cares about such things.

Unique only to me, I like that line, because that's the most important thing, Me!

Woman, as she thought to herself.
"Me, Woman"
How unique is that, born second.

~ ~ ~ ~ ~

I looked at the one born first, "Man, Oh Man, Oh Me, Oh My!"

Sometimes I think I was born knowing what to do; vaguely remembering having to do any studying on this awesome specimen.

I looked upon his skin as it glistened in the dark, the moon cascading over his lower extremities; his legs built like the pillars upholding the palace.

I could probably hold up only one at a time, barely, I'm sure I would be unable to lift him.
Beautiful creatures they are, born Man, born first. But he was just one of many.

~ ~ ~ ~ ~

Born woman,

I was given a good memory and that's why I've made it a point to live my life with excitement... it started with the apple... and man is now a part of that excitement.

Life would have been boring without him. Not always understanding his words, I listened for his heart.

At times, expressionless when I needed him to love my naked soul more than my naked body.

I've since come to realize that only I was born loving my Naked Soul... others would have to learn.

~ ~ ~ ~ ~

I find men fascinating not just their physical being but the essence of his soul. Even before he was close enough, I could smell him with my eyes.

They all seem to be that way to me, each one stood out above the rest; each one in present in his time and secure in that space. (a certain Gena???)

His smile, his lips, his tilt, the way he watched me when I licked and bit my lip. The way he so gingerly kissed the curvature of my hips; his lips pressed against mine, it's time for a skinny dip. He bites me on my ass, I say don't move so fast. Enjoy the ride, make it last!

Born woman, I'm glad.

I say don't move so fast. Enjoy the ride, make it last! Born woman, I'm glad!

~ ~ ~ ~ ~

The car arrived to pick us up. Single and surfing, we were riding the wave.

I knew when we were introduced that our souls had connected.

As our eyes met I looked away, as I had done so often, but it was too late.

I knew at that moment we would meet again.

~ ~ ~ ~ ~

Born woman I shall live an eternity!

My life was anything but typical, gifted with intuition I was born with intrigue, and thirst for excitement.

Born to Love man, I did. But I also loved me. Life has afforded me the opportunity to say, "It's My Pleasure" and mean it!

Each moment I enjoyed. My friends laugh when I say, "I've had so many wonderful orgasms, I could be having one right now". Batting my eyes could cause a tsunami.

Born woman, loving your self brings the greatest rewards.

I can determine who will share my space.

His scent in the atmosphere, I get close and inhale. And again I take a breath, he's present and attentive. I feel the heat of his lips as I caress his occipital ridge.

Born woman with a good memory!
Make every thought count, if it's not
worthy disregard it!
I remind myself.

~ ~ ~ ~ ~

Born woman. I awake to another day
to arrange.
The phone rang, I answered and a
sweet low voice said, "Hello".

A smile appeared immediately on my
face. I'm sure he would hear the
smile in my voice, as I answered with
another long hello. I closed my eyes
and took a breath.

How's the writing coming along?

This fine piece of specimen asked. Drifting, I responded, "Great, free flowing".

He was my current muse, and sometimes sweaty inspiration.

It was a rainy night, and I found myself not long after his phone call standing at his front door. My sexy open toe stilettos now filled with mud, as I tried to take my short cut across the grass. Who would dare to wear such sexy shoes out in the rain?

Born woman with pretty feet and an awesome pedicure, that would be me, at his door step... He opened the door with that cheesy smile. Looking down at my feet, I tell him, "You may want to grab some towels I wouldn't want to track mud through your house".

He dashed off, and back with a quickness placing them on the floor as I walked to the nearest seat to the door.

He removed my shoes, walked into the kitchen and returned with a warm towel and began wiping the mud off my feet, between each toe nice and slow.

Completely clean, he finished them off with a soft kiss and a pair of socks.

Man the one born first, treating me like a queen I had no problem shucking the corn for my king. Dinner Served.

~ ~ ~ ~ ~

I simply will not be bored with my romantic, orgasmic, thought provoking memories. I can't imagine maturing without them. Born woman, we've each been given our own unique experience in life! I've enjoyed and still enjoying my experience, living in the present, reflecting on the past, that is impacting my future.

Man the one born first, stretching me to love more! ~ Born Woman

~ ~ ~

So now just a few examples of how you can take various concepts, and styles to create your book!

Your Book Launch!

Now that you've made the investment in writing your book, I would hope that you're ready for a return on your investment.

In the SBB full service package for authors, we assist you in designing a campaign for your book launch; along with creating your brand page to successfully market your book through social media.

There are a variety of social media networks that can link you to potential consumers. Here are the top six:

Foursquare   Google   Twitter

Linkedin   YouTube   Facebook

Facebook, YouTube, and Linkedin rank the highest for active users. Presently Facebook has 1.39 billion active users, and according to current studies, more users tend to access the brand they're interested in, via social media more so than the brands websites.

More and more television commercial ads are incorporating facebook, #hashtags, and twitter into their campaigns.

Due to Social Media users are more likely to try new things, or read a book, based on the suggestion of a friend; and they tend to stay more engaged with the brands they like.

The value of social media is presently indisputable; consumers are going to talk anyway, but the advantage you have with a brand page is the opportunity to control the message that goes out.

Now STOP...if you haven't already joined the "Writing a Small Bite Book!" group on Facebook do it now. Send us a private message with your email and we'll send you a Free Report with tips on using social media.

Why use Social Media to Build your Brand?

- ❖ Grow Your Fan Base
- ❖ Create Engagement
- ❖ Build Relationships with Members
- ❖ Create Affiliate/Advocates
- ❖ Provide Exclusive Offers
- ❖ Allows Fans to Share the Experience
- ❖ Build Trust with Followers
- ❖ Discover Your Tribe

You can maximize your marketing efforts by launching the same campaign throughout several of the networks. You must have a strategic plan to keep your followers/fans engaged.

By keeping your followers connected to the message, they are more likely to share it.

This is a huge benefit to building your brand as it increases word-of-mouth advertisement, and brings a greater awareness to who you are and what you have to offer.

This will drive traffic, and attention to your brand. So you've got to get your followers to actively like, share, subscribe, and connect. Now STOP ...join our group and share it with your friends, and let them know that you just may become the next featured SBB Author.

Social profiling is also on the rise which means you can strategize your marketing by aggregating the information about consumers across the different social networks; employment history, education level, and more.

With this information you could create unique quizzes and surveys that can help you to collect high-quality leads; giving you a larger conversion, and greater retention.

With Google at your fingertips and sites like Survey Monkey, creating survey's and quizzes can be simply done.

Ok, we're getting close to the end, and I hope you've been brainstorming, and writing down some notes the entire time you've been reading this book. If you're a first time author, you should be ready to make the call for a free consultation.

Creating a Visual Video Vibe!

"Doing your thing on video"…will simply allow your followers and potential followers, to get to know who you are.

Video is part of our daily lives whether you're watching television, or a YouTube channel. With the increase of digital cable, video on demand, and satellite to the already existing commercial and public television systems; the number of available channels has increased dramatically.

The introduction of inexpensive, yet high quality (HD) video equipment has given new authors an advantage to gaining a greater amount of exposure. You could choose to do your own or hire a videographer to produce a book launch trailer, and or a series of reports leading up to your launch. Not to mention future training programs, and educational webinars for eLearning.

As an author, launching your book you want to be prepared for interviews, panel discussions, and or you could be invited to be on a talk show. Whatever the format it's important that you're able to communicate effectively on video. SBB authors who select the full service package receive a manual on Communicating on Video, and free access to "Doing Your Thing on Video" training videos.

Here are a few tips to help you see how valuable this training could be for your campaign.

The editorial format can be used on public access television, or internet broadcasting. The presentation is a prepared statement directed to a viewing audience; because it's usually designed to be brief, you must choose words and information carefully.

You can minimize your mistakes by having a small production team with a copyright editor, lighting and camera technician; which will help you produce a higher quality presentation.

Cameras can be intimidating and this will affect your presentation. Be sure to sit straight, but relaxed in your chair, visualize a good friend and speak naturally.

Your appearance in a video is very important, in the appendix of our manual "Doing Your Thing on Video," you'll find tips on gestures, clothing, your speaking voice, and more.

Developing your skills for speaking on video could open up an opportunity for you to become a frequent guest on a variety of programs; such as talk shows, radio, live stream, and podcast which will garner you even more exposure.

You must anticipate questions and prepare your responses. Most of your professional interviewers will provide you with a few basic questions ahead of time.

During the interview be enthusiastic, stay calm, listen carefully, be authentic, and never rush to give an answer.

In our manual we have more tips, and assignments that will help you create winning interviews, and there's a lot more that we cover with our SBB authors, such as talk shows with an audience, the press conference, and fielding questions from your radio audience.

Small Bite Books is simply here to enrich your overall book writing experience. Be sure to connect with us on Facebook, like our page... and let's take the next small step together!

I'll leave you with this:

Visibility + Value

+ Consistency

= Influence

That's the Law of Familiarity, stay connected with your followers by creating relevant, valuable products that can improve their lives.

~ ~ ~

Success Perpetuates Success ~

You're Up Next!

Other Books by Jo Grace

Learn how creating a Space of Grace with Anointed oils can enhance your spa experience... this Hands~On therapy can Support Emotional & Physical healing! Written by a Certified, Master Educator ~ Jo Grace

My Story

As a child I always loved reading the Readers Digest that was usually placed on the tables to read at the doctors or dentist office. Somehow that particular childhood memory has remained with me, which explains my love for books; most of them being personal, spiritual, biblical, and business development.

Over the years I have acquired, read, studied, and taught from my share of books. My family and friends would probably share their experience of having to move them; they weren't to happy when they lifted an extra large tote bin filled with my books. That day I learned to transport my books in apple boxes, if I had any hopes of them ever helping me again.

About the Author

According to her 1st grade teacher, Jo Grace had already begun demonstrating her dramatic communication skills, but her teacher wanted her to do it in a quieter manner, so she would have her write her story's, then let her share them with the class.

In 2009, Jo Grace inspired by her early years of reading short stories in the Readers Digest during her doctor visits, decided to create her own concept for Small Bite Books. Being the entrepreneur that she is, her journey didn't stop there. She began to look at how she could use her skills to help develop other aspiring authors by creating a Short-Cut to Success using Small Bite Books.

But she discovered that after the books were written there was more to be done...

Capturing the essence of your message, Jo Grace, along with her business partner, Victor Irving Jenkins founded Crave the Spotlight Media Marketing in August 2011. Her fifteen year background as a master educator made her very effective in developing online training courses for Educators and Coaches. As a radio host she developed her skills for interviewing authors, speakers, coaches and other business professionals; she has been effective on both sides of the camera. As the director of photography, Jo Grace touts the use of video in marketing, monetizing your message and telling your story. CTS is the leading online media provider for Speakers, Educators, and Coaches. Video is one of the fastest growing online marketing and SEO strategies. She utilizes her exceptional editing skills and eye for aesthetic appeal to produce state of the art products for her clients. Her meticulous attention to detail permeates the entire company.

Secrets of a Sexy SuShi!

An Affirming Book For the Creative Feminine Leaders of Tomorrow!

She Uses what She has for Her own Inspiration!
Jo Grace

Don't have a whole lot of time to read, this is a great gift for you or some busy person you know! ...this book is an easy read with affirmations for women, young and mature who need to discover or rediscover their SuShi! SuShi stands for... She Uses what She has for Her own Inspiration! A SuShi is a woman excited about her own femininity; she turns herself on...instead of waiting for others to do it for her. She loves herself, her butt, her eyes, and even her thighs; regardless of the size! And if she's not quite happy with it, instead of sitting around whining and complaining, she makes happen the things in life that she wants! This is an Apple-tizer as it was designed for and published by Small Bite Books. When you're ready for the entire meal connect with ~ Author Jo Grace @ Facebook. Book for Speaking, or private Coach sessions. Purchase at Amazon.com/author/jograce

"Raising SuShi's"

Learn How to Empower Yourself &

Impact the Lives of Your Daughters!

Customized for small or large events!

Learn How to Become Your Brand @

"Business Secrets of a Sexy SuShi"

For a schedule of upcoming events,

connect on Facebook

www.facebook.com/jograceupclose

Send email to:

jograceupclose@live.com

Be sure to type

Secrets of a Sexy SuShi in Subject box.